Proveen
servicios

por Marianne Lenihan

Scott Foresman
is an imprint of

Glenview, Illinois • Boston, Massachusetts • Chandler, Arizona
Upper Saddle River, New Jersey

Every effort has been made to secure permission and provide appropriate credit for photographic material. The publisher deeply regrets any omission and pledges to correct errors called to its attention in subsequent editions.

Unless otherwise acknowledged, all photographs are the property of Pearson.

Photo locations denoted as follows: Top (T), Center (C), Bottom (B), Left (L), Right (R), Background (Bkgd)

Opener: ©DK Images, (C) ©Royalty-Free/Corbis; 1 (CL) Comstock Inc., (CR) ©Royalty-Free/Corbis; 3 ©DK Images; 4 ©DK Images; 5 ©DK Images; 6 ©DK Images; 7 ©Royalty-Free/Corbis; 8 Comstock Inc.; 9 ©DK Images; 10 ©DK Images; 11 (BL) ©Royalty-Free/Corbis, (C) ©DK Images; 12 ©DK Images

ISBN 13: 978-0-328-53443-2
ISBN 10:   0-328-53443-9

1 2 3 4 5 6 7 8 9 10 V0G1 18 17 16 15 14 13 12 11 10 09

Una comunidad es un grupo de personas. Las ciudades y los vecindarios están formados por comunidades.
Las personas de una comunidad cooperan y hacen cosas juntas para evitar un caos. ¿De qué comunidades formas parte tú?

La comunidad se beneficia de sus miembros de maneras diferentes. En una ciudad, mucha gente ayuda a la comunidad con su trabajo. Proveen un servicio. Por eso se llaman trabajadores de servicios. ¡Veamos cómo ayudan los trabajadores de servicios!

Los oficiales de la policía patrullan sus comunidades en carro, en bicicleta o a caballo. Se aseguran de que todos estén a salvo. Algunos policías dirigen el tráfico. Todos los policías ayudan a los miembros de la comunidad a vivir juntos en paz y seguros.

Los bomberos apagan incendios en sus comunidades. Los camiones de bomberos llevan escaleras y mangueras sujetas al camión. Los bomberos se ponen ropa especial, máscaras y cascos para rescatar a quienes estén dentro de un edificio en llamas. Si hay personas quemadas, las atienden hasta que se las llevan al hospital.

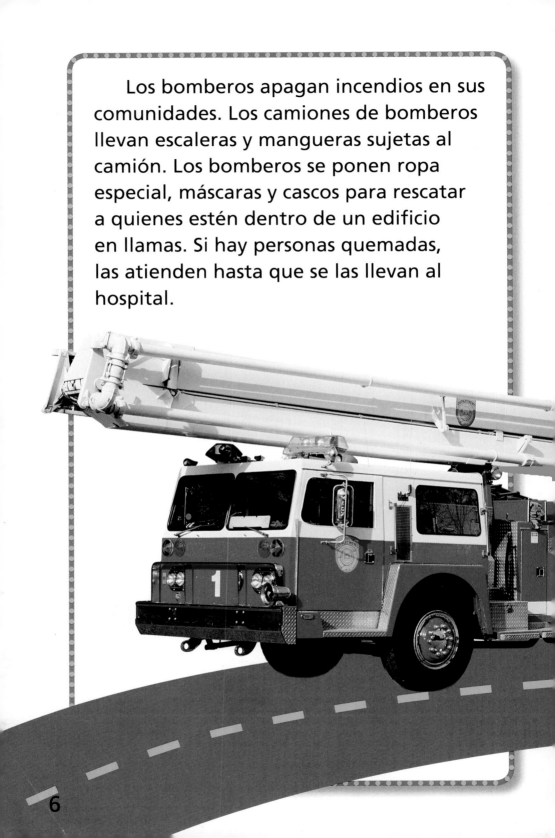

Cuando suena el rugido de la alarma en la estación de bomberos, los bomberos se suben rápidamente al camión de bomberos. Los camiones van a toda velocidad hacia el incendio. Cuando llegan, apagan el incendio con sus mangueras.

Los maestros y los entrenadores también son trabajadores de la comunidad. Tus maestros te ayudan a aprender. Te pueden enseñar a leer y a escribir. Los entrenadores te ayudan a aprender a practicar deportes. También te enseñan a jugar de manera justa con otros.

Los doctores y las enfermeras nos ayudan a mantenernos sanos. Cuando estamos enfermos o heridos, nos caemos o golpeamos, los doctores y las enfermeras nos ayudan a sentirnos mejor. Los doctores y las enfermeras pueden trabajar en hospitales y en clínicas.

Los trabajadores de primeros auxilios también nos ayudan si estamos enfermos o heridos. Nos llevan rápidamente al hospital en sus ambulancias. Todos los días los trabajadores de primeros auxilios salvan vidas en nuestras comunidades.

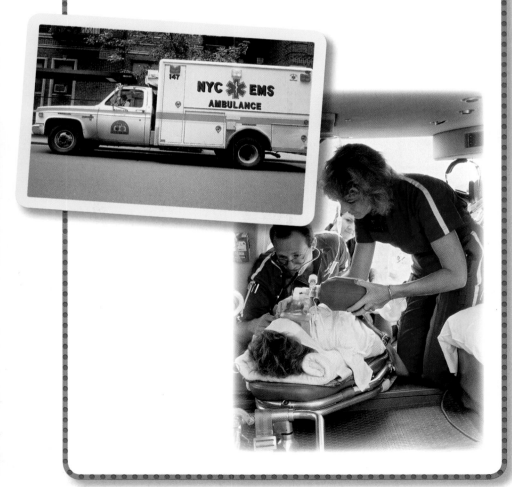

Los empleados de correos trabajan en la oficina de correos. Ayudan a sus comunidades encargándose del correo. Los carteros llevan el correo a las casas y a los lugares de trabajo. ¿Quién te trae el correo?

Probablemente conoces a un bibliotecario de tu escuela o de tu biblioteca local. A los bibliotecarios les encanta leer y nos ayudan a encontrar información y libros.

Las comunidades están formadas de personas que coexistimos juntas y nos ayudamos. ¿Qué otros trabajadores de tu comunidad puedes loar o elogiar? Nómbralos.

Spanish
is my
Superpower

Bien

Amor

Hola

Adiós

Si

Por Favor

Jennifer Jones

Spanish
is my
Superpower

Jennifer Jones

I start each day looking out the window.
I say, "Buenos diás," to the sun.
I hope whatever happens
My day is filled with fun.

I go and greet mi perro,
Patting him gently on the head.
He barely even looks up,
Wagging his tail from his doggie bed.

Mi mamá and mi papá are up.
"Buenos diás!" they both say.
I give them a hug and kiss.
Then I get on the bus and go on my way.

At home, we speak mostly Spanish,
But sometimes I speak English when I'm out.
I'm lucky to be fluent in both languages.
I can speak and understand both, no doubt.

My thoughts are mostly in Spanish,
But I used to hardly speak Spanish aloud.
Even though it's my native language,
Speaking it used to not make me proud.

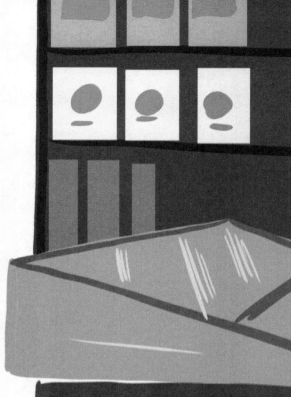

¡Las manzanas se ven bien!

I used to be afraid that speaking Spanish
Made me different and stand out.
But I've learned to be proud of my heritage
Because it's what I'm all about!

One day at school, a kid arrived.
She didn't know much English and was new.
I helped her out because I remembered,
Kindness starts with you.

I offered my hand to her and said,
"¿Como estás?" and she replied, "Bien!"
The other kids asked, "What does that mean?"
And we had the chance to teach them.

They all wanted to learn some words,
Like please and thank you.
We told them it's por favor and gracias.
They thanked us for teaching them, too!

As it turns out, my best friend saw this incident,
And the principal at our school.
They came over, gave me a high-five and said,
"Hey, that was very cool!"

I started to think about my family —
My abuela, my primas and primos, as well.
I realized being able to speak to them
Was actually pretty swell!

The next day, I went to school.
I said, "Hola!" to everyone in sight.
It made me feel good inside,
Being proud of my heritage just felt right.

Hola

Being bilingual is special.
It opens up a whole other world,
Where I can communicate confidently,
With so many other boys and girls.

I couldn't wait to get home,
And speak Spanish to my mom and dad.
I told them about my day at school.
They were so surprised and glad.

I'm proud I can speak Spanish.
It's not something everyone can do.
Speaking Spanish means there are so many more people
Who you can speak to and understand you!

I'm so happy I finally learned,
What it took me so long to see,
That Spanish is my superpower,
And an important part of being me!

I love to hear from my readers. Write to me at jenniferjonesbooks@gmail.com

Please visit chairsonstrike.com for the latest news and updates on future titles!